JIM
AND THE
RED TAILS

JEREMY P. ÄMICK

TULSA

ISBN: 978-1-957262-46-8
Jim and the Red Tails

Yorkshire Publishing
1425 E 41st Pl
Tulsa, OK 74105
www.YorkshirePublishing.com
918.394.2665

Published in the USA

For my friend Jim: may your story of service with the
Tuskegee Airmen continue to inspire generations to come.

During World War II, Black Americans volunteered to serve the country,
Saying goodbye to those they loved at home to join the military.
It was a time of segregation, when some citizens were denied basic rights,
Yet bravely went to combat and revealed their dedication in the fight.

Inspirational was their service, but challenges back home remained.
Even though these Tuskegee Airmen went on to boldly earn their fame.
The world would hear of their missions and how they did prevail,
Because of those like Jim Shipley, a crew chief for the "Red Tails."

Born in the town of Tipton, Missouri in the summer of 1923,
He had many white friends with whom he played in the streets.
Jim went to Harrison School, where the local Black children did learn,
With his father as teacher—a man both educated and firm.

Although sickly as a child and having troubles catching his breath,
Jim gained strength and learned the value of hard work and sweat.
He was taught to work on engines and shined shoes at a local store,
While his father instilled a sense of faith, attending church was never a chore.

Back in the 1930s, Black students did not have a high school in town,
So young Jim decided to go to work and a mechanic job he soon found.
Gaining automotive skills that benefitted him in the years to come,
When he worked on many aircraft that helped preserve our freedoms.

In 1942, a recruiter inspired Jim to consider changing his course,
Saying the U.S. military was working to form an all-Black Air Force.
Passing the tests, he trained in Alabama at a place called Tuskegee,
Recalling, "There were Black soldiers everywhere, as far as you could see."

For the next few weeks, the soldiers fired their rifles and learned to survive.
While groups of young Black pilots flew planes high in those Alabama skies.
Then on to Nebraska, where Jim learned to fix fighter planes,
Like the P-40 Warhawk, that gained frontline battle fame.

At Selfridge Field in Michigan is where he spent the next several weeks,
Working everyday with his pilot and checking his plane for oil leaks.
On weekends off they went to town, enjoying dances and dinners,
While their chances for combat deployment seemed to grow dimmer.

But the adventure began for Jim and the 332nd Fighter Group
When they departed the United States aboard large ships made for troops.
They soon arrived in Italy as part of their country's army,
Conducting patrols and strafing missions against the enemy.

Jim and the crews maintained their airplanes in prime condition,
Using their tools and knowledge to keep the pilots safe on their missions.
They witnessed Mt. Vesuvius erupt near Naples, Italy.
The only active volcano in Europe, and quite the sight to see.

They moved to another Italian airstrip and received P-47 Thunderbolts,
A new airplane with the speed and power to give the enemy a jolt.
But the Black pilots were not trusted by the Army or given good missions to fly,
Until Colonel Benjamin O. Davis said, "We can perform, let us take to the skies!"

It was to another airfield in Italy, where Jim and the airmen then moved,
And their dominance in the combat zones they continued to prove.
The Black airmen escorted the white bomber pilots, guarding their flanks,
While piloting their sleek, new and quick P-51 Mustangs.

14

The Mustangs' tails were painted bright red by Jim and the ground crews,
So American bombers knew it was them when they came into view.
The Tuskegee Airmen earned another great name, becoming the Red Tails,
Protecting the bombers from attack, accomplishing this duty without fail.

Sometimes the Red Tails did return with bullet holes in their wings,
And Jim would patch the damage with metal cans and similar things.
Harry Stewart was one of Jim's pilots, who learned to fly when in his teens,
He shot down three enemy planes on one mission, making his Mustang sing.

Maintaining the planes was important, pilots needed the crews backing,
To be ready for the next mission, where great courage was never lacking.
When the German forces finally surrendered on May 8, 1945,
The Red Tails celebrated the victory, although some friends did not survive.

They began to turn in their planes, ready to go back to their loved ones,
And boarded a troopship bound for home since their job overseas was done.
Jim received his discharge with no further military duty to serve,
Returning to Missouri to visit his family and go back to work.

He soon made a trip to Kansas City and planned to visit with his sister,
Wearing his military uniform, looking forward to some time with her.
While there he stopped by an ice cream shop but was told that since he was Black,
They could not serve him in the front, he would need to go around back.

He served overseas, supporting combat missions to help free other people,
But here in the United States, these Black soldiers were often not equal.
There would unfold many civil rights efforts to ensure all could be free,
Equal rights inspired by the Black troops who served in the military.

The Red Tails showed they were among the finest of the country's troops,
Of which their successful record in combat became the best proof.
As years passed by Jim went to work, fixing trucks for a local company,
And then met Mildred, who became his wife, and they started a family.

The community heard of Jim's service with the famed Red Tails,
Seeking to learn more about their accomplishments in greater detail.
The Tuskegee Airmen received several awards for all of their achievements,
And Jim explained to audiences the story of their past treatment.

The men of the Red Tails never relaxed and in their lives went to great lengths,
To share what they had done, a demonstration of their courage and strength.
Jim remains a humble man who knows that the war was not easily won,
Fortunate that all put aside their differences, learning to work "together as one."

CPSIA information can be obtained
at www.ICGtesting.com
Printed in the USA
BVHW021934201022
649899BV00020B/668